Rex to the rescue

Story written by Gill Munton
Illustrated by Tim Archbold

Speed Sounds

Consonants   *Ask children to say the sounds.*

f ff ph	l ll (le)	m mm mb	n nn kn	r rr wr	s ss se c (ce)	v ve	z zz se s	sh	th	ng nk

b bb	c k ck	d dd	g gg	h	j g ge	p pp	qu	t tt	w wh	x	y	ch tch

Each box contains one sound but sometimes more than one grapheme.
*Focus graphemes for this story are **circled**.*

Vowels

Ask children to say the sounds in and out of order.

a	e ea	i	o	u	ay a͡-e	ee ea y e	igh i͡-e ie i	ow o͡-e o
at	hen	in	on	up	day	see	high	blow

oo u͡-e ue	oo	ar	or oor ore aw	air are	ir ur er	ou ow	oy oi
zoo	look	car	for	fair	whirl	shout	boy

5

Story Green Words

Ask children to read the words first in Fred Talk and then say the word.

Luke   Bruce   Sue   Duke   cute   lead   brute   rage   growl
snarl   mule   stroke   truce

Ask children to say the syllables and then read the whole word.

tatt|oo   vel|vet   coll|ar   mi|nute   ma|roon   acc|use   stubb|orn

---

Ask children to read the root first and then the whole word with the suffix.

pounce → pounced   choke → choking   escape → escaped

refuse → refused   chase → chased

6

Vocabulary Check

Discuss the meaning (as used in the story) after the children have read each word.

	definition:	sentence:
tattoo	a pattern made in ink on your skin	The big man with the shaved head and the tattoos.
minute	tiny	Not so much little as minute!
maroon	dark red/purple colour	This smart lady in the maroon skirt is Sue.
brute	a bully	"Shoo, you horrid brute!" said Luke.
refused	didn't want to do something	She refused to listen.
stubborn	refuse to give in, determined	Big Dude was as stubborn as a mule.
truce	end of a fight	I want all the dogs to call a truce.

Red Words

should	were	there	call
want	come	could	one
through	was	you	to
said	all	of	through
any	some	does	are

Rex to the rescue

This is Luke. He's the big man with the shaved head and the tattoos.

The little pug with the blue velvet collar is Luke's dog. His name is Bruce. Cute, isn't he? He's not so much little as minute!

Luke likes to take Bruce to the park. Bruce chases sticks (well, twigs) and barks at the ducks, while Luke sniffs the roses or reads 'Gardening Today', humming a little tune.

This smart lady in the maroon skirt is Sue,
with her dog, Duke.
Duke's a bulldog – a big brute with sharp teeth.

One day last June

Sue took Duke to the park.
Luke and Bruce were there, too.

Sue let Duke off the lead.
Duke sniffed the ground – he could smell dog!
Then he was off, zooming across the grass.
Past the slide, past the roundabout, past the swings,
until he was nose to nose with Bruce.

"Shoo, you horrid brute!" said Luke,
choking with rage.
It was no use – Duke started to growl
and snarl.
Then he pounced on the poor pug.

Sue came running up.

"Kiss Mummy, Dukey darling!" she said.
"He's in a bad mood today.
The postman escaped before Dukey
could bite him."

"That's no excuse!" said Luke. "Bruce isn't used to fighting.
He's only had one fight in his life – and that was with a hamster.
Bruce lost!"

Just as Luke was sniffing a prize bloom and Bruce was having a snooze on his fluffy blanket, Duke came back.

This time, he chased Bruce all round the park.

"I don't want to be rude," said Luke to Sue, "but that dog should be kept on a lead."

Sue refused to listen.
"Don't you accuse darling Dukey!" she snapped. "Come on, Duke!"

The next day

This little girl is Luke's pal, Fran.
This huge brute is
her dog, Rex.
He's a bull mastiff!

Rex was as stubborn as a mule.
So when he spotted Duke – and chased
him across the grass, up the slide, round
the roundabout, over the swings and *right into
the lake* – Fran couldn't stop him.

"Thank you!" said Luke to Fran.
He stooped to stroke Rex.

"Good boy!" he said.
"I want all the dogs to call a truce.
No more fighting! Okay?"

"Yep!" barked Bruce.

"Yep!" barked Rex.

"Sploosh!" barked Duke,
through a mouthful of green slime.

Questions to talk about

Ask children to TTYP each question using 'Fastest finger' (FF) or 'Have a think' (HaT).

p.9 (FF) Which word describes the size of Bruce?

p.10 (HaT) What is scary about big Duke?

p.11 (HaT) How do you think little Bruce felt?

p.12 (HaT) Why do you think Sue wasn't cross with Duke?

p.13 (HaT) Why did Luke think Duke should be kept on a lead?

p.14 (FF) Where did Rex chase Duke?

p.15 (HaT) Why was Luke thankful to Fran?

(FF) What did Luke ask the dogs to do?

Questions to read and answer

(Children complete without your help.)

1. What is Luke's dog like?

2. What does Duke do to Bruce?

3. Why was Luke cross with Sue?

4. What does Rex do?

5. What is the truce at the end?

Speedy Green Words

likes	tune	use	June
nose	bite	rude	listen
take	name	thank	smart
teeth	before	fighting	life
right	skirt	little	across